MW00445006

Happy Coloring!

Heather Land
HEATHER'S ADULT COLORING BOOKS
www.HeatherLandBooks.com

THIS BOOK BELONGS TO:

_____

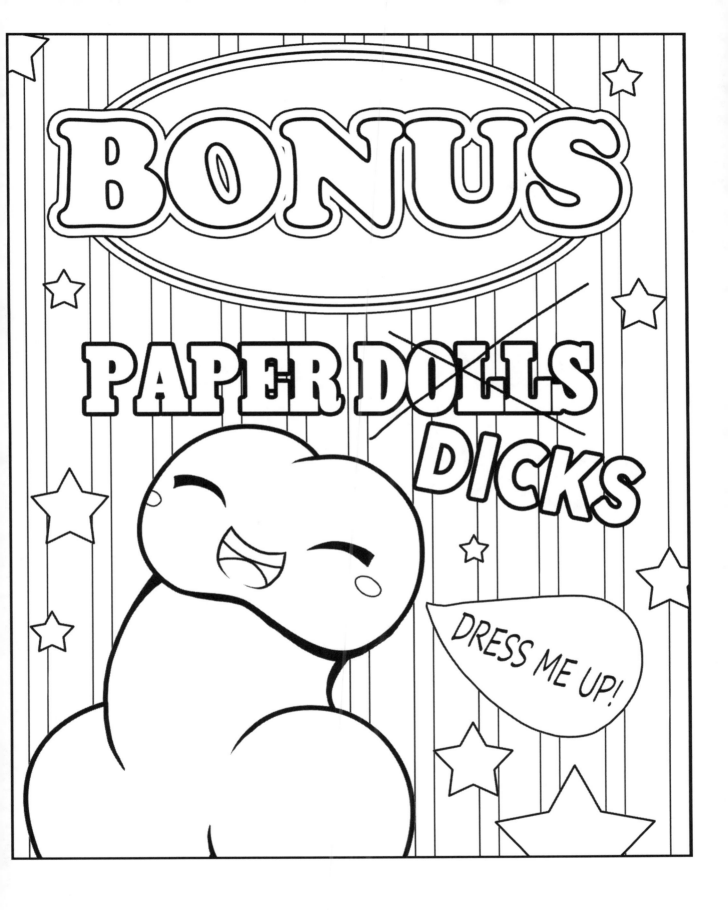

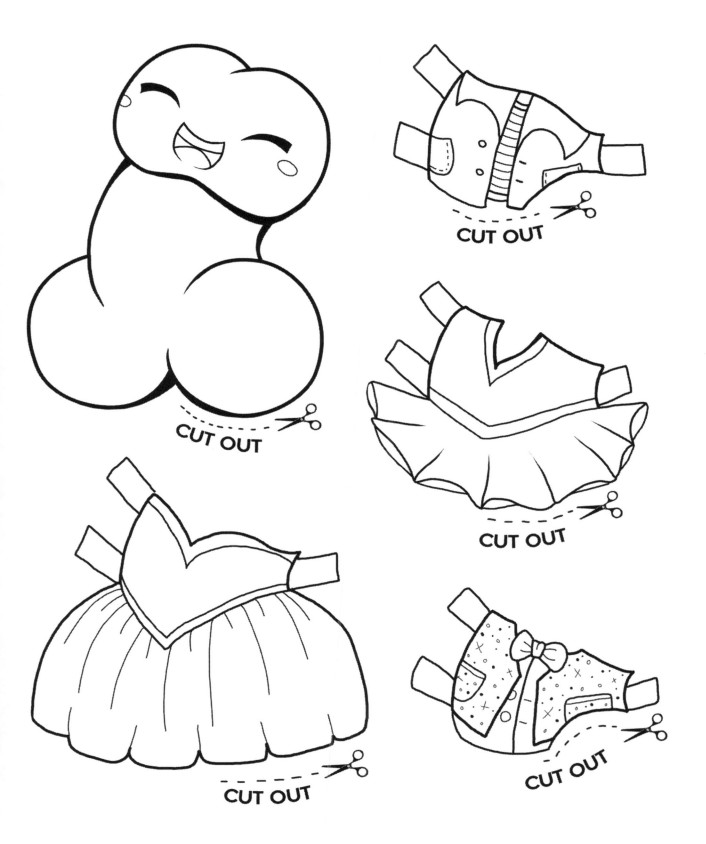

CUT OUT

CUT OUT

CUT OUT

CUT OUT

CUT OUT

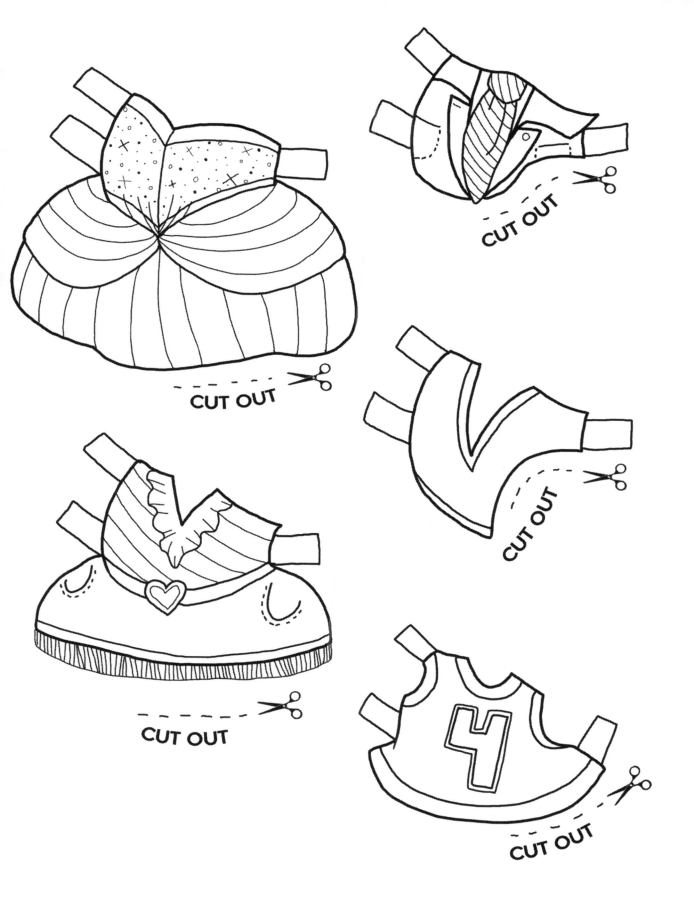

CUT OUT

CUT OUT

CUT OUT

CUT OUT

CUT OUT

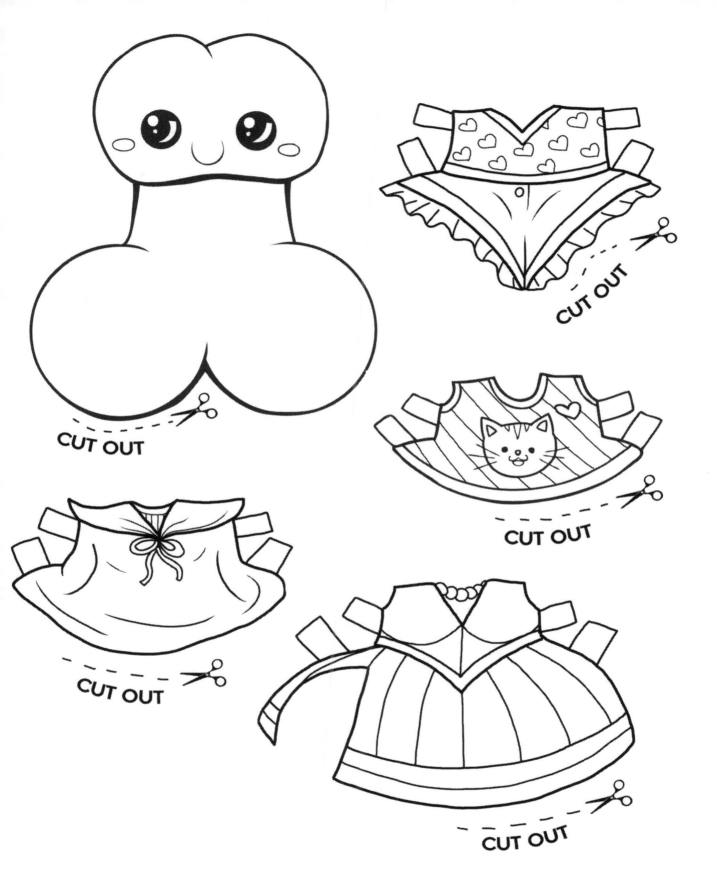

CUT OUT

CUT OUT

CUT OUT

CUT OUT

CUT OUT

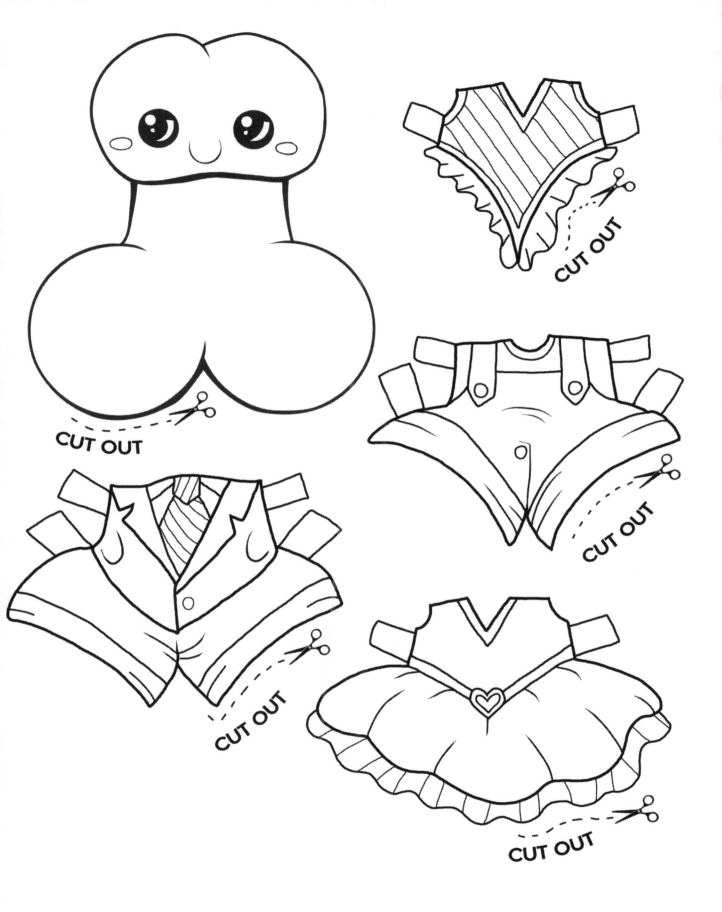

CUT OUT

CUT OUT

CUT OUT

CUT OUT

CUT OUT

COLOR TEST DICKS

TEST YOUR COLORS HERE
BEFORE COLORING EACH PAGE

COLOR TEST DICKS

TEST YOUR COLORS HERE
BEFORE COLORING EACH PAGE

COLOR TEST DICKS

TEST YOUR COLORS HERE
BEFORE COLORING EACH PAGE

Made in the USA
Coppell, TX
10 November 2023

24040381R00039